You Can Put Out The Fire Inside You By Writing

Signature :

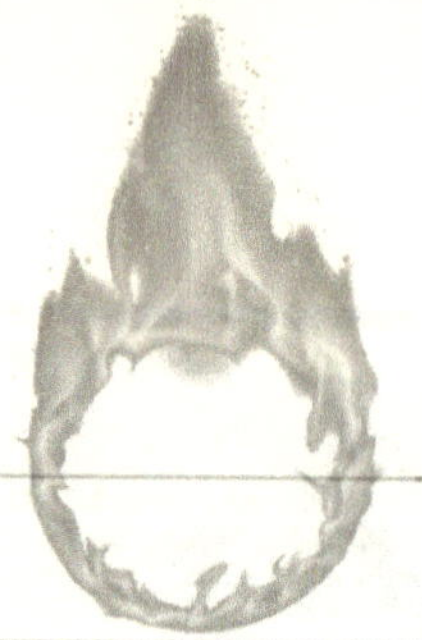

Date : / /

Date: / /

Date: / /

Date: / /

Date: / /

Date: / /

Date : / /

Date: / /

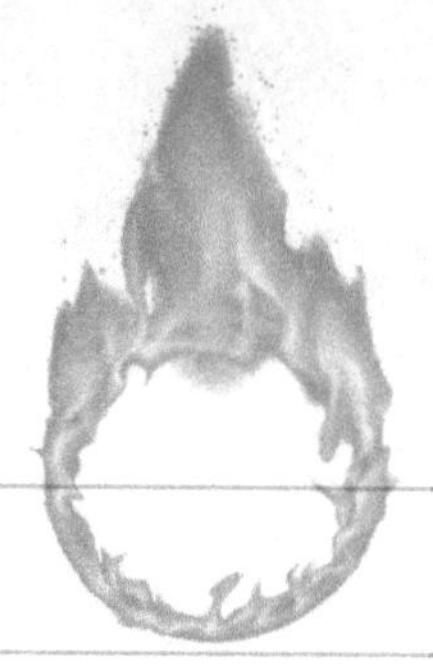

Date : / /

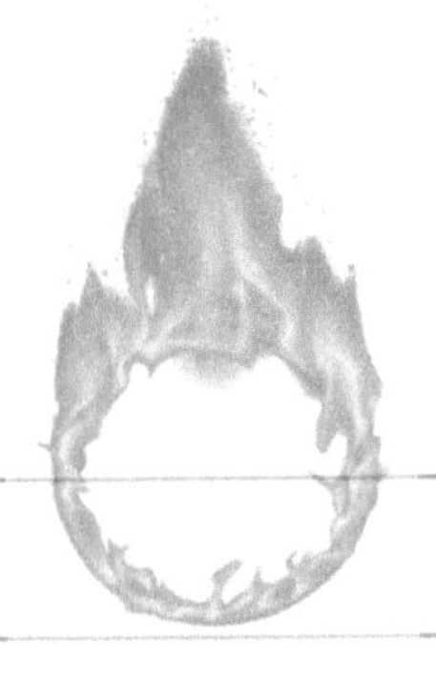

Date: / /

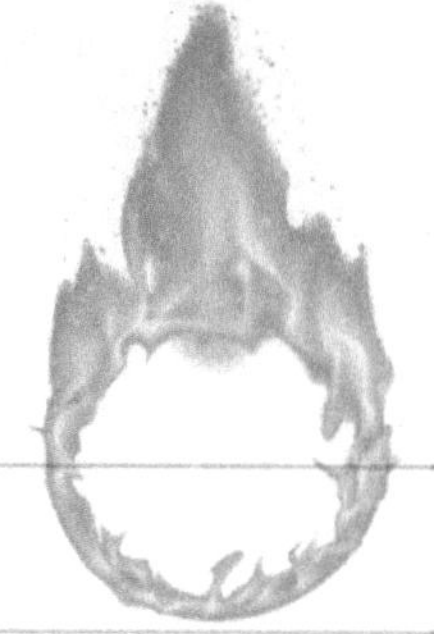

Date : / /

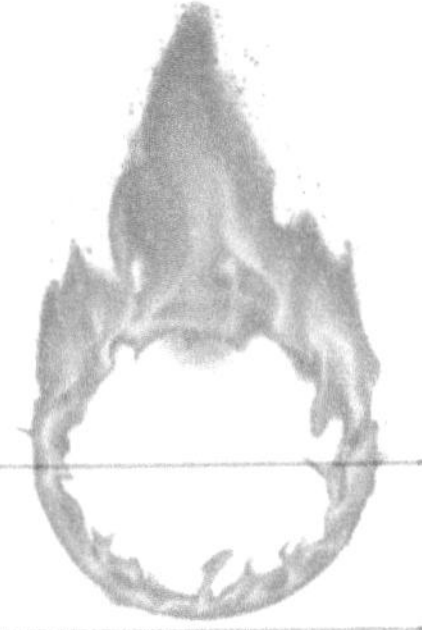

Date: / /

Date: / /

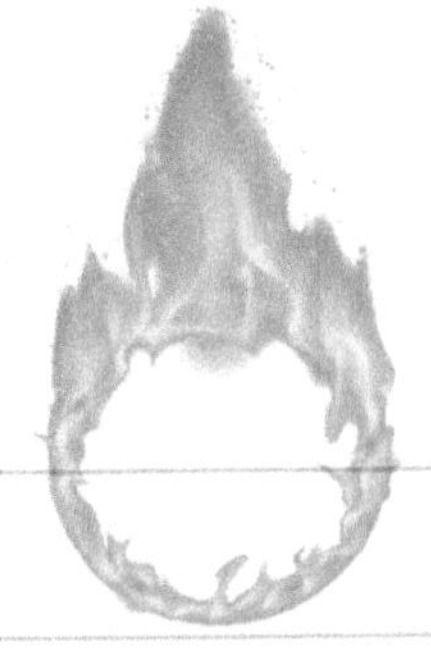

Date: / /

Date : / /

Date: / /

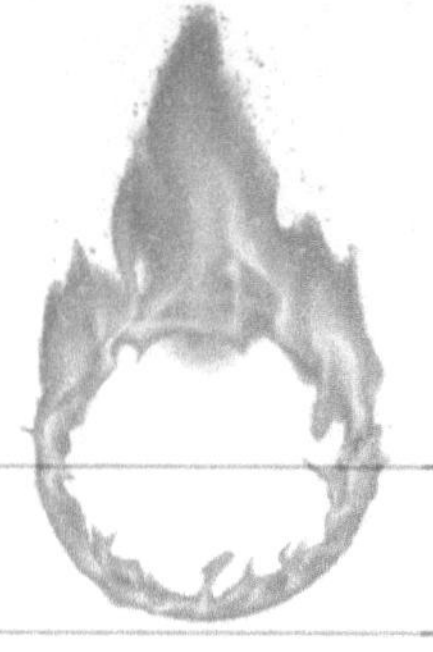

Date : / /

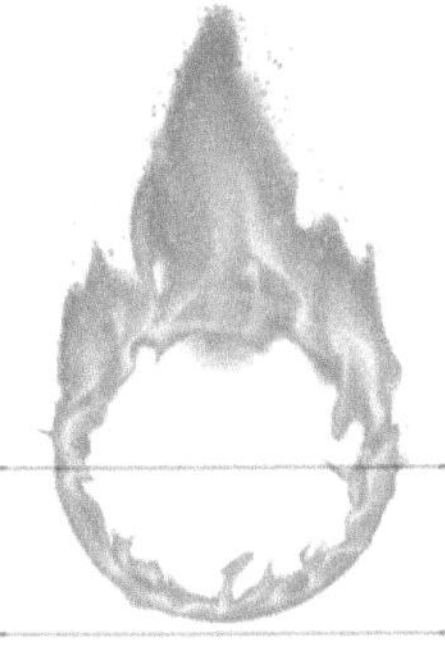

Date: / /

Date: / /

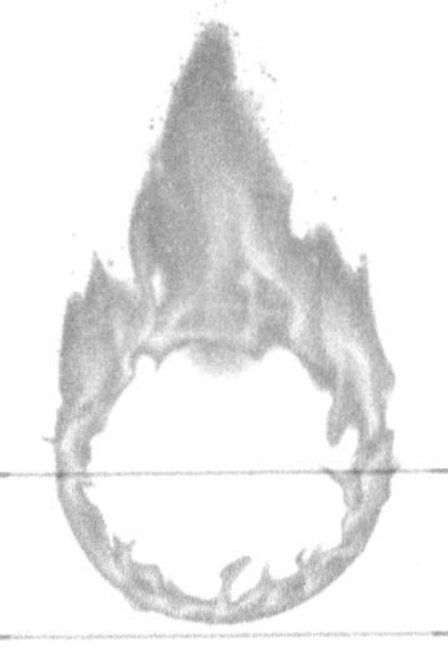

Date: / /

Date: / /

Date: / /

Date : / /

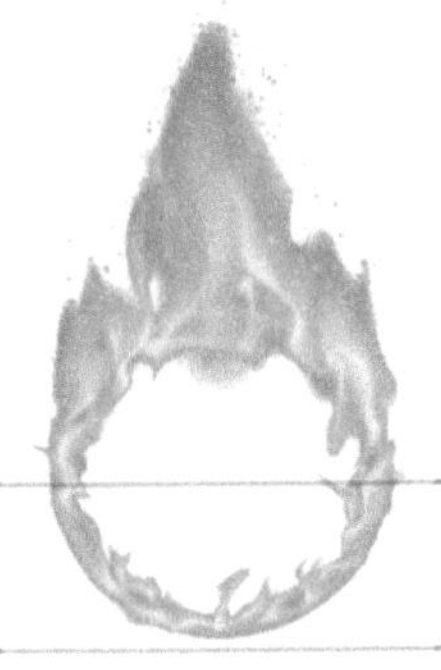

Date: / /

Date: / /

Date: / /

Date : / /

Date: / /

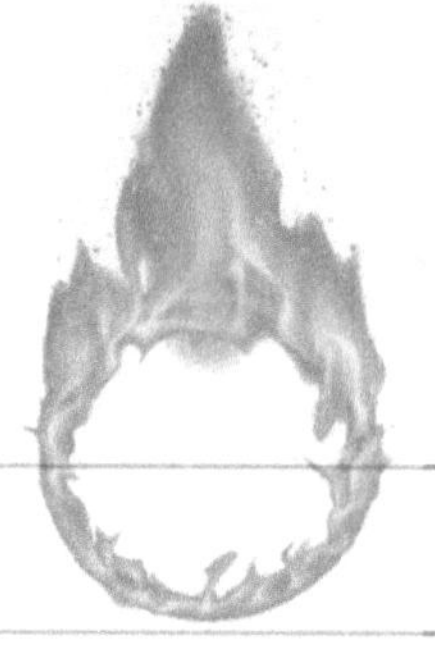

Date : / /

Date: / /

Date: / /

Date: / /

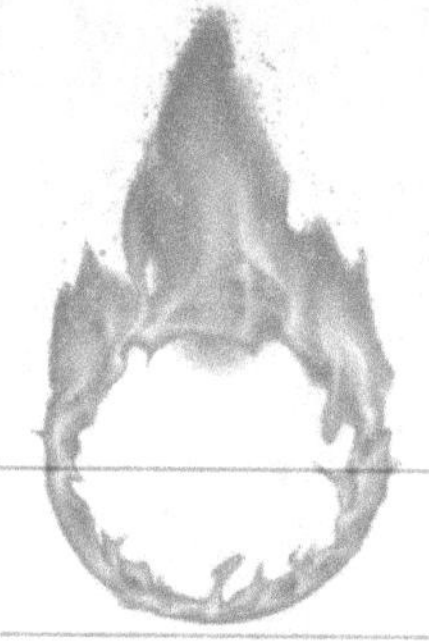

Date: / /

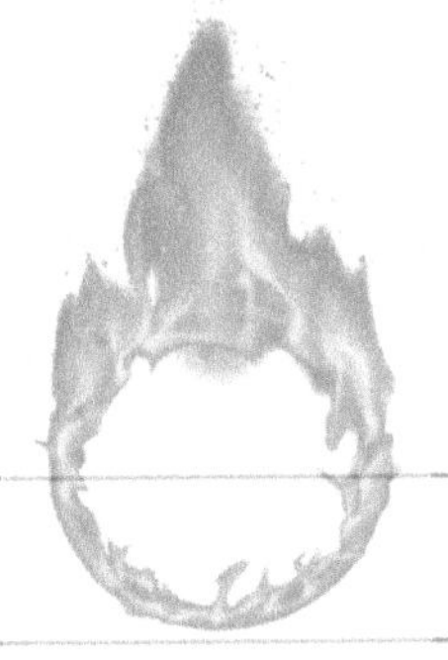

Date: / /

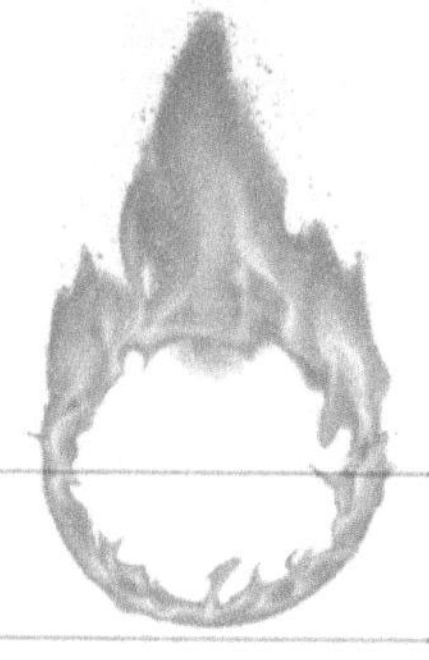

Date: / /

Date: / /

Date: / /

Date: / /

Date : / /

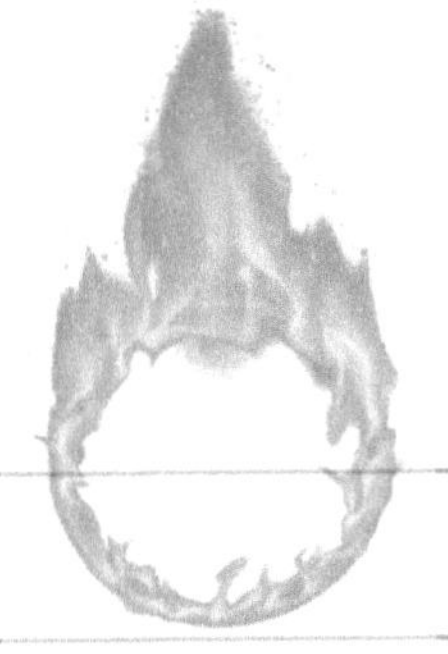

Date: / /

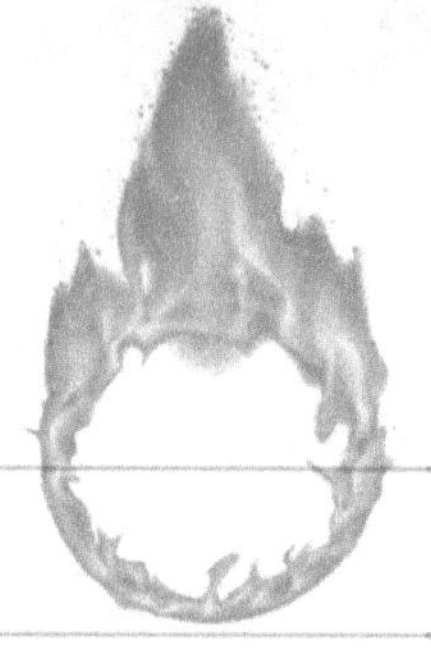

Date : / /

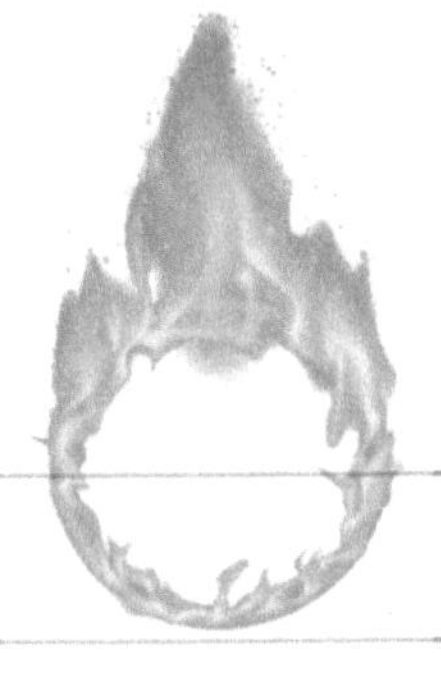

Date : / /

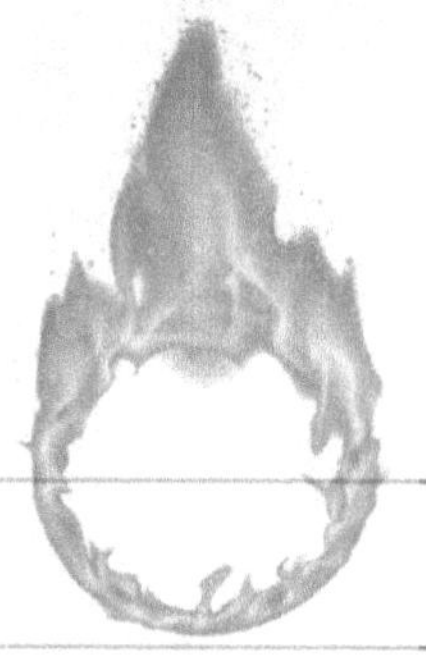

Date: / /

Date: / /

Date: / /

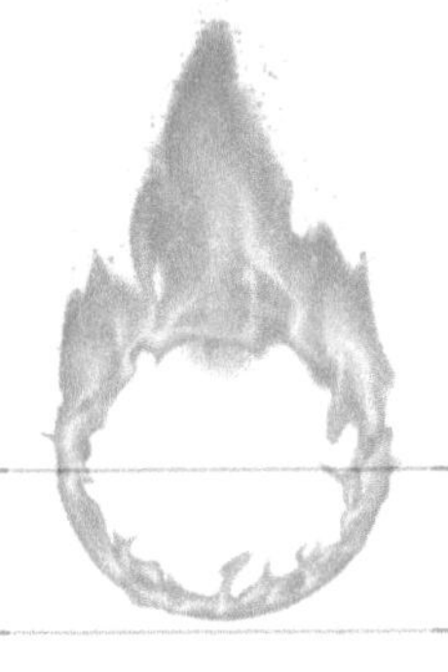

Date: / /

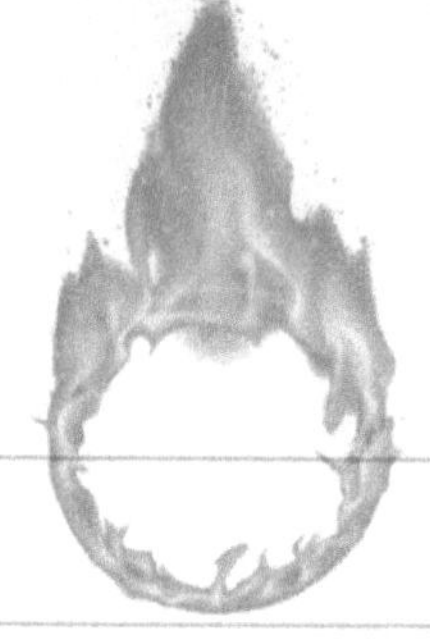

Date: / /

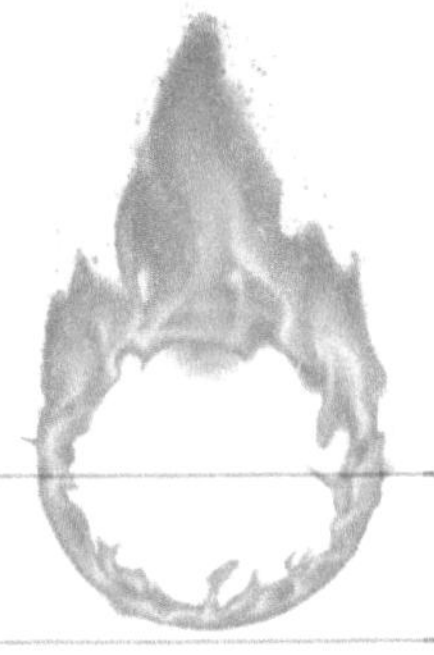

Date: / /

Date: / /

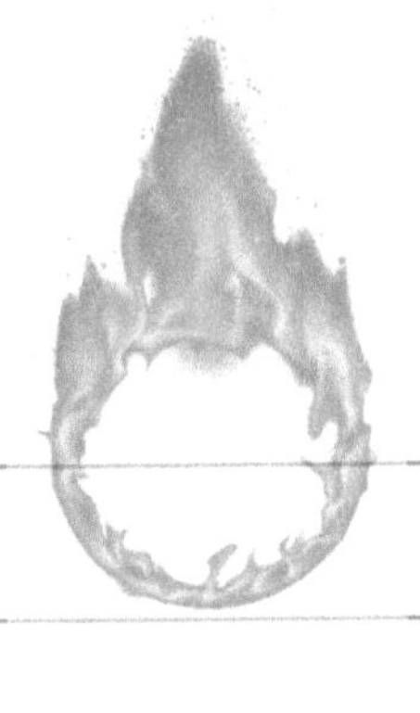

Date: / /

Date : / /

Date: / /

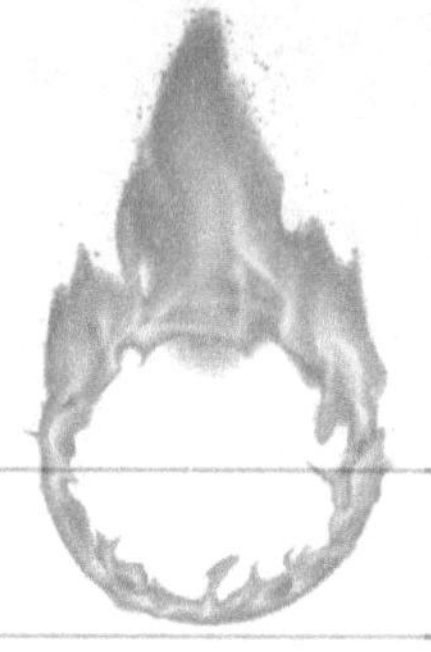

Date : / /

Date: / /

Date : / /

Date: / /

Date :   /   /

Date: / /

Date: / /

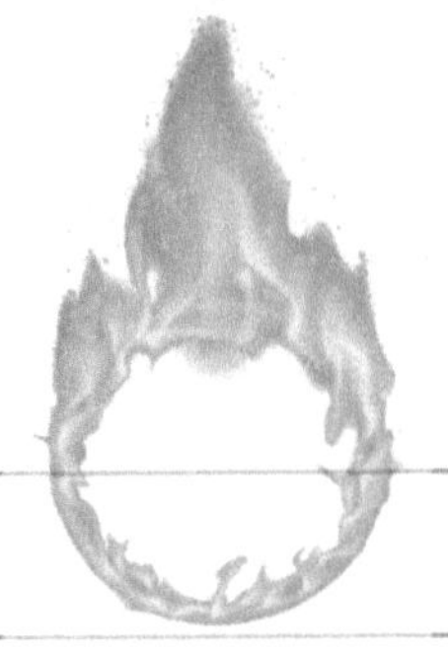

Date: / /

Date : / /

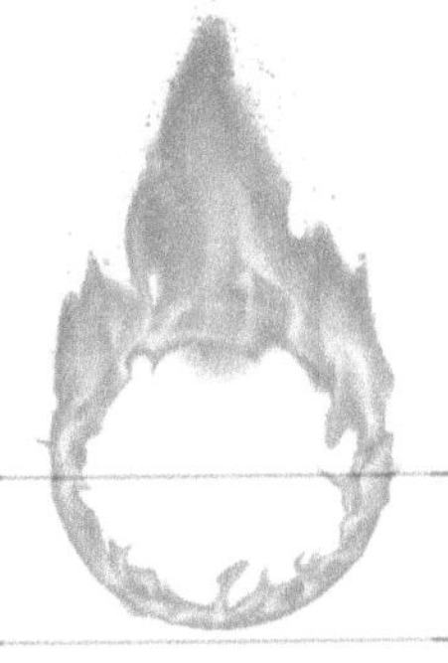

Date: / /

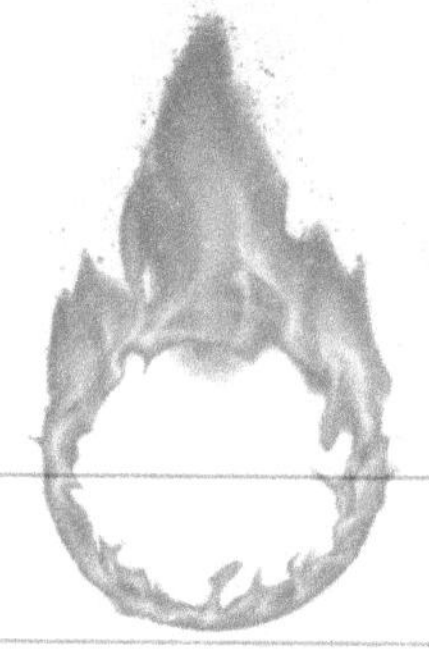

Date: / /

Date: / /

Date : / /

Date : / /

Date: / /

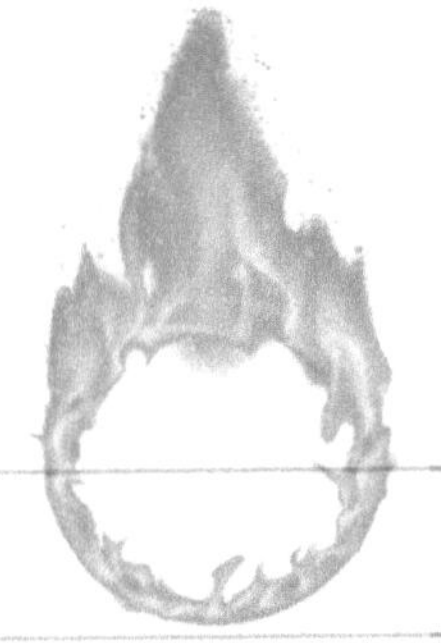

Date: / /

Date: / /

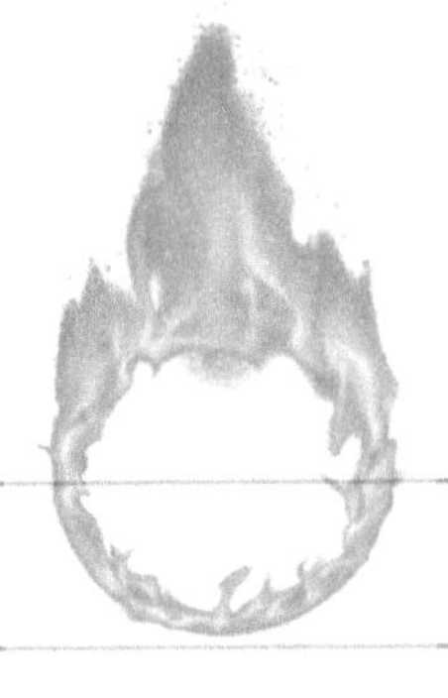

Date: / /

Date: / /

Date: / /

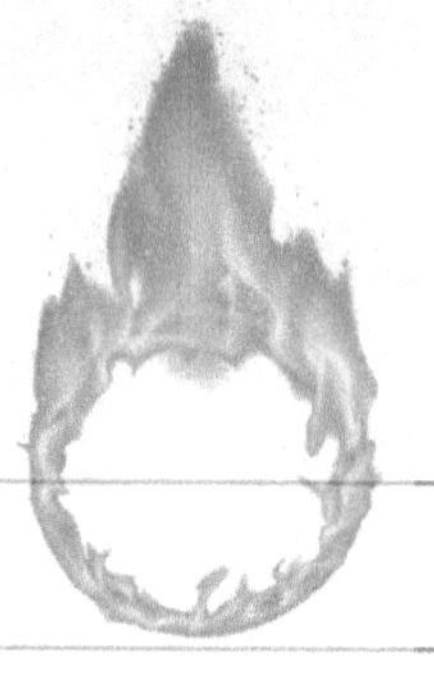

Date : / /

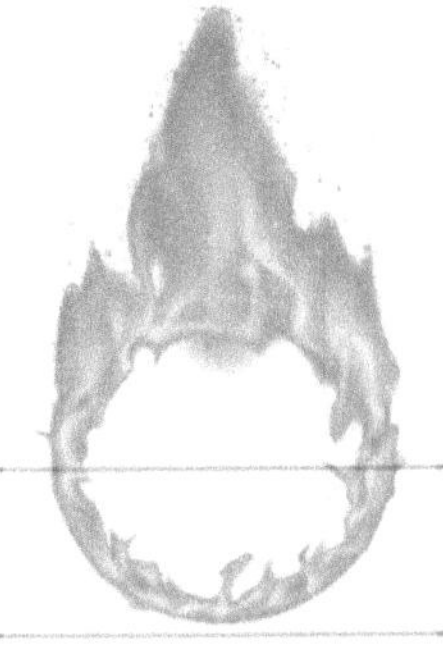

Date: / /

Date: / /

Date: / /

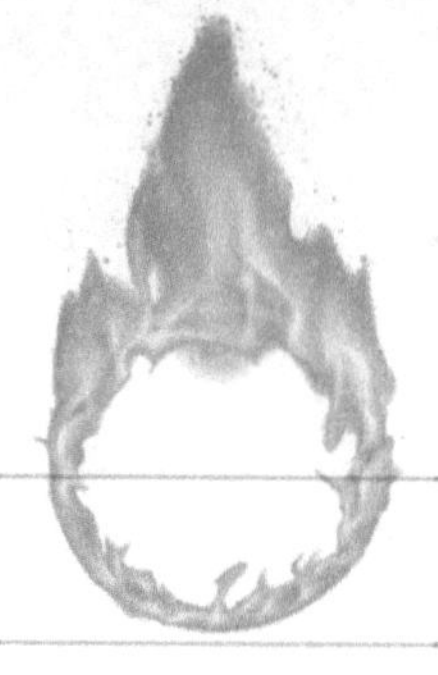

Date: / /

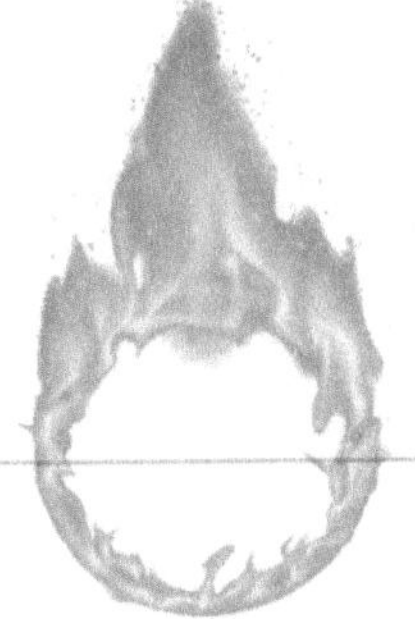

Date : / /

Date: / /

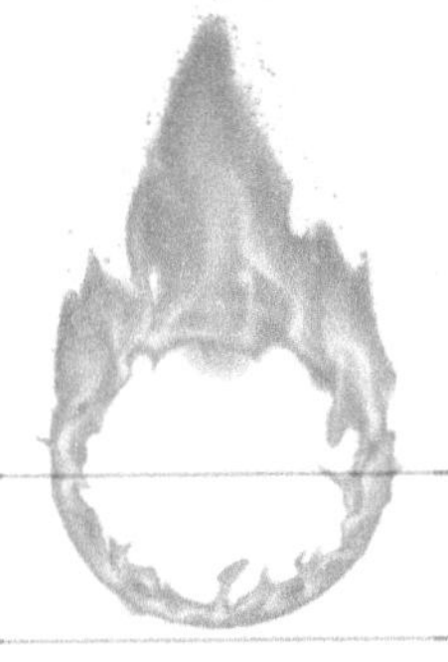

Date: / /

Date: / /

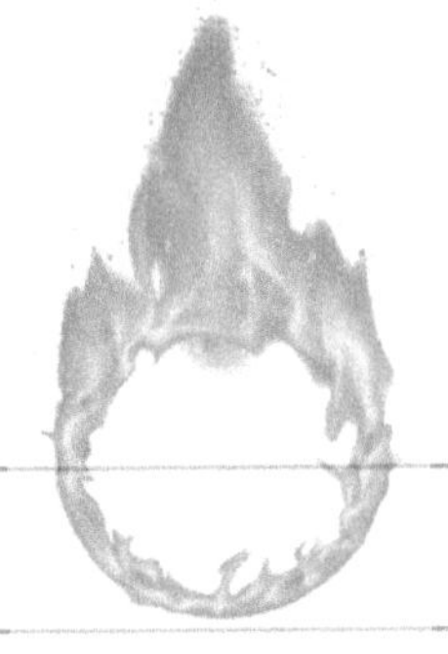

Date: / /

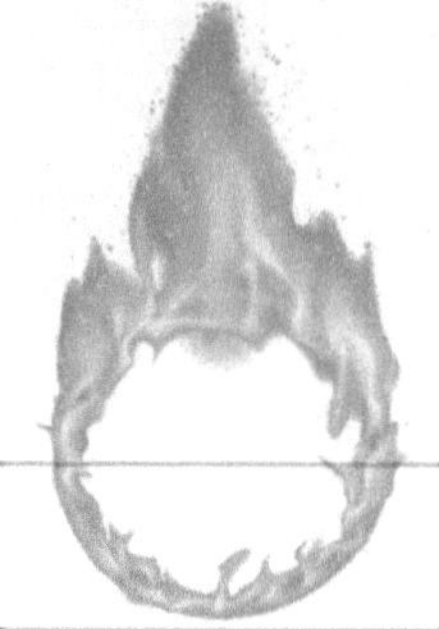

Date : / /

Date: / /

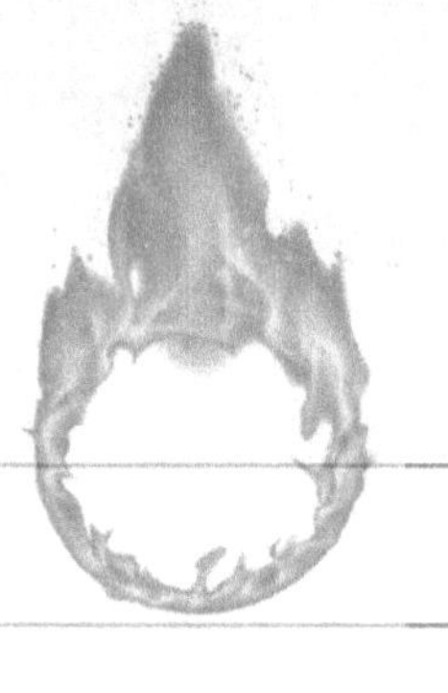

Date: / /

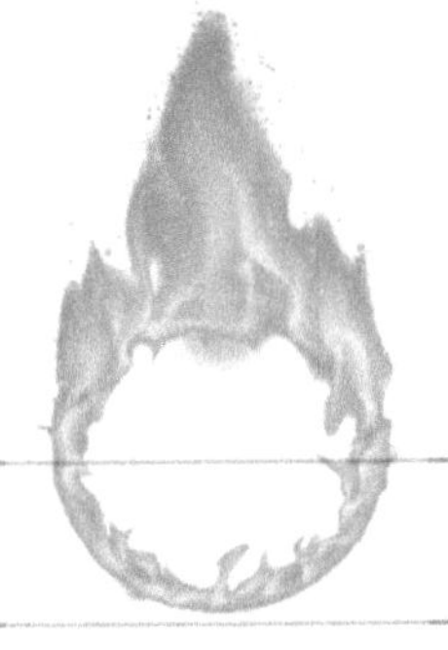

Date: / /

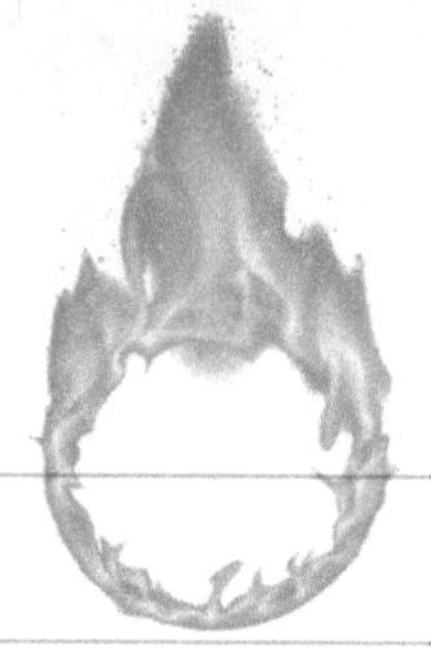

Date : / /

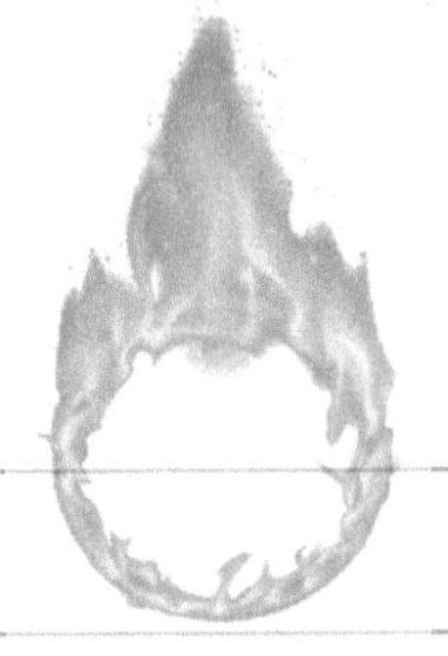

Date: / /

Date : / /

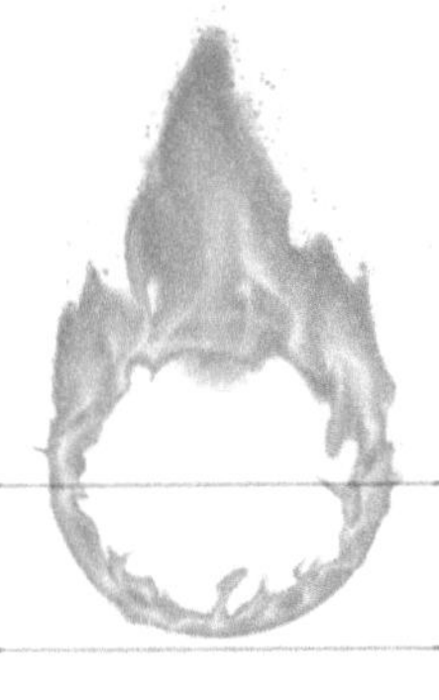

Date: / /

Date: / /

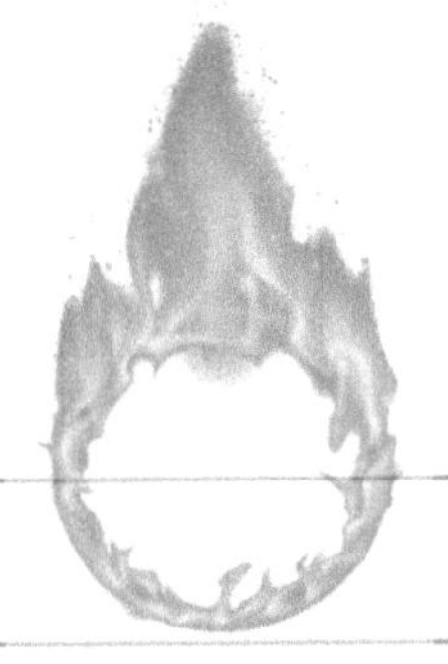

Date: / /

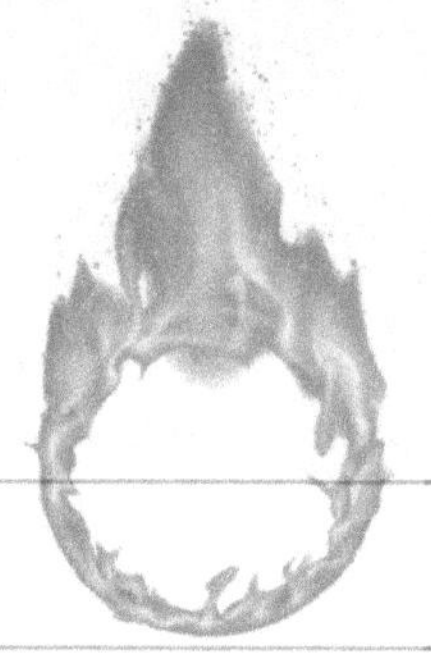

Date : / /

Date: / /

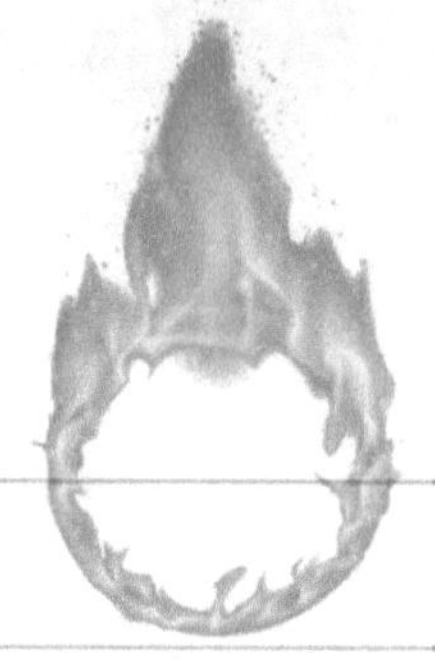

Date : / /

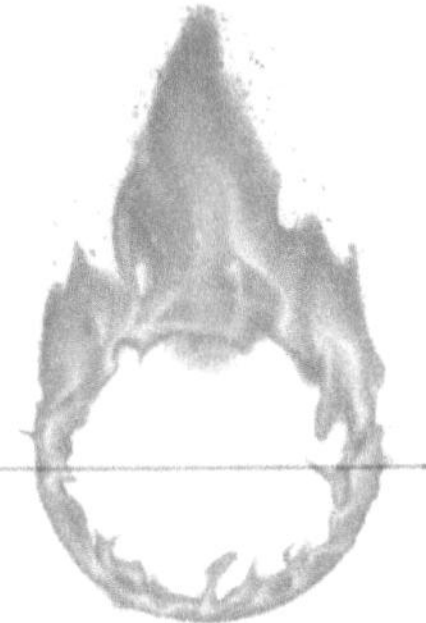

Date: / /

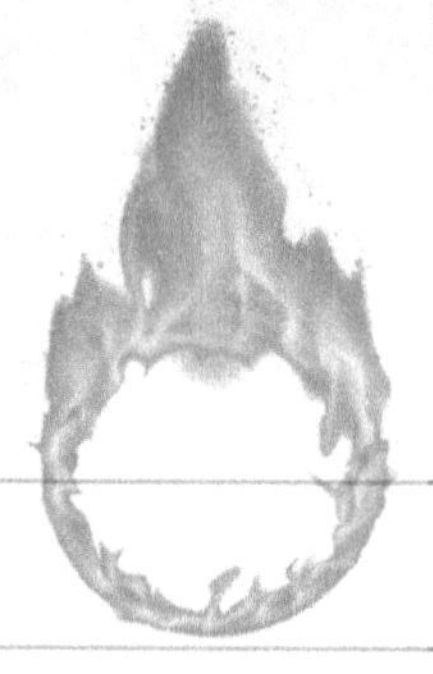

Date: / /

Date: / /

Date : / /

Date: / /

Date : / /

Date: / /

Date : / /

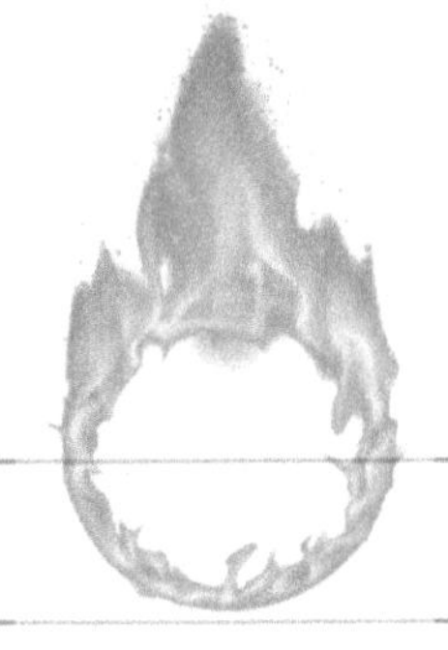

Date: / /

Date: / /

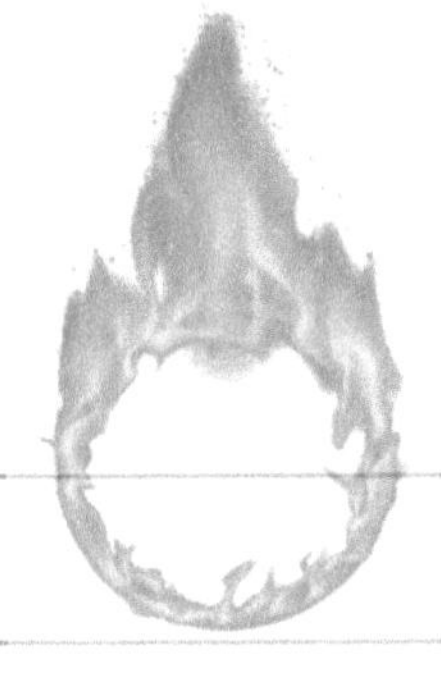

Date: / /

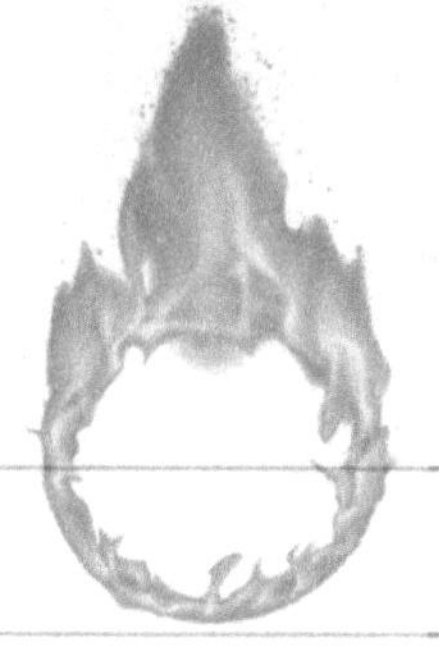

Date : / /

Date: / /

Date: / /

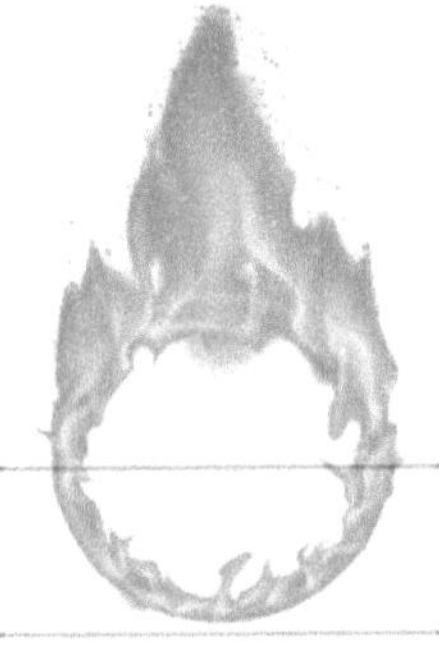

Date: / /

Date: / /

Date: / /

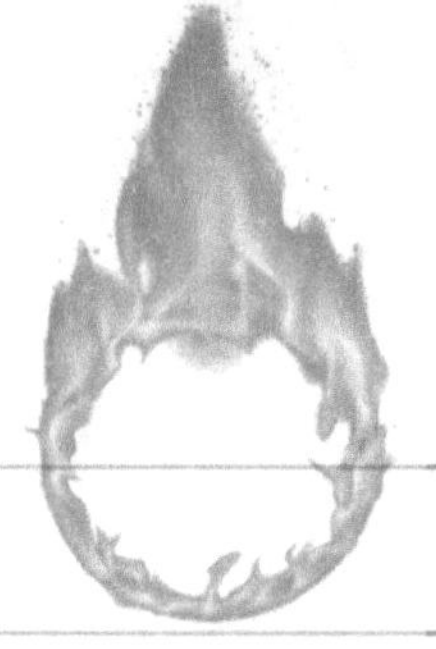

Date: / /

Date: / /

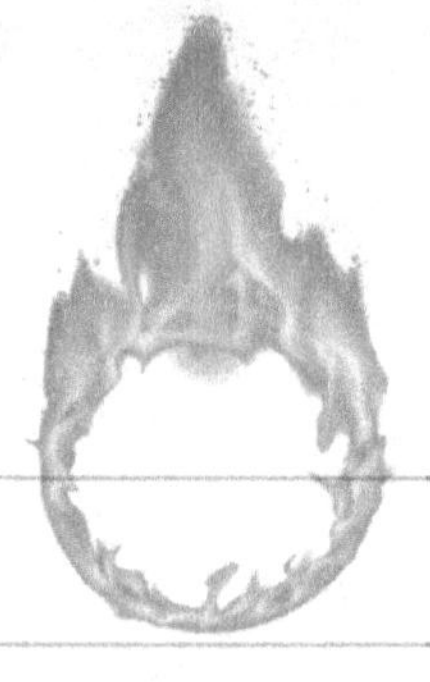

Date: / /

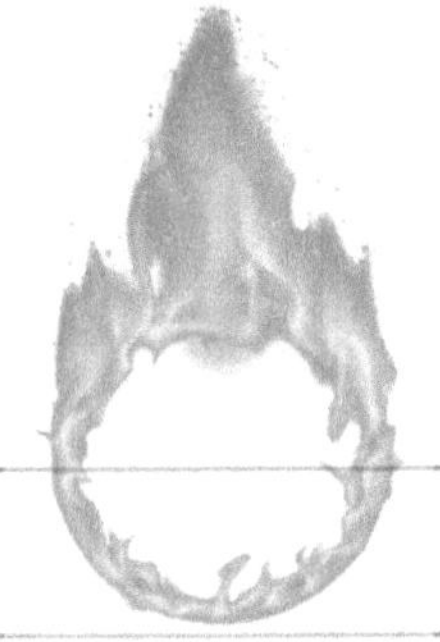

Date: / /

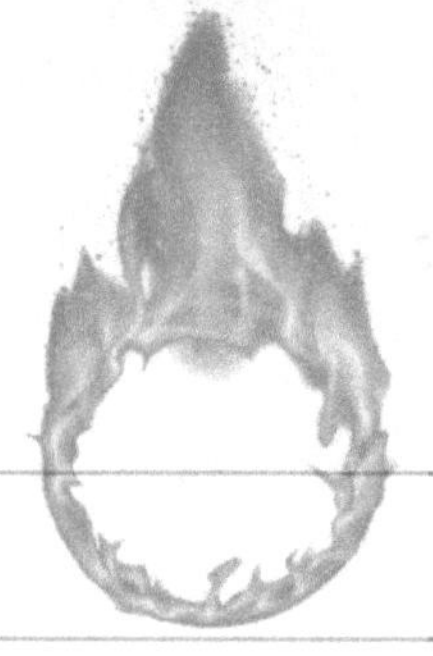

Date: / /

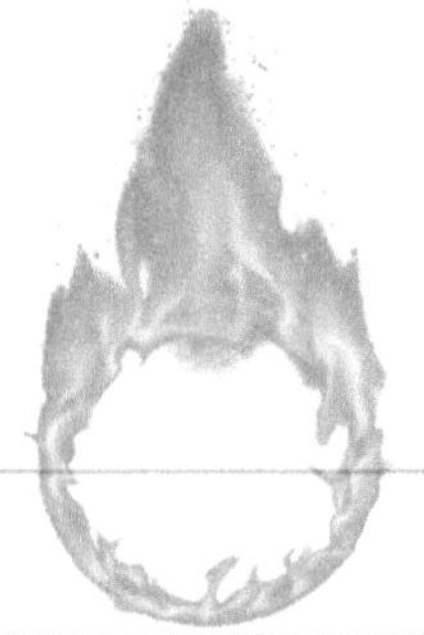

Date: / /

Date: /   /